DEC 0 4 2017

SPOTLIGHT ON ■ Russia

Written by Sue Reid

Contents

Collins

Introduction
Twice the size of Canada!

Russia is the biggest country on the planet, measuring about 10,000 kilometres from east to west. It's twice the size of Canada, the world's second largest country. To travel all the way across, you go through 11 time zones. Some of the coldest inhabited places are in Russia, while others are very hot. Once a vast empire with a single ruler, the country is now a **federation** of regions and **republics**. The capital is Moscow.

Moscow is an ancient city, with lots of new buildings, too. Not everyone likes the new developments.

In the far north of Russia, people have to dig or scrape holes in the ice to fish during winter.

Chilly!
The coldest town on Earth, Verkhoyansk, is in Russia. Would you like to play outside when the temperature is –60 degrees centigrade?

European or Asian, or something in-between?

There are around 140 million people living in Russia. They belong to many different ethnic groups, some of which have their own languages.

Modern Russians are descended from the Slavic and Rus tribes who settled in the country around 1,500 years ago. The word "Rus" gives us the name "Russia". As their country is in both Europe and Asia, Russians sometimes wonder whether they are European or Asian. Nobody has ever really been able to decide.

> Some parts of Russia are in Europe, and others in Asia. People think that the Ural Mountains mark the border.

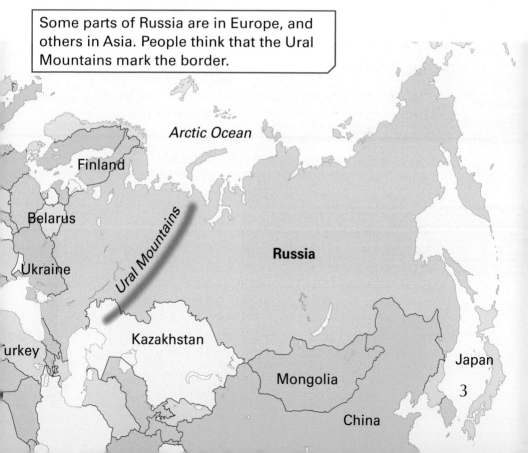

3

Russia's history

Ivan the Terrible

Russia didn't become one country until the 1550s, when it was united under the first **tsar**, known as Ivan the Terrible. He drove out the Mongols, invaders who had ruled parts of the country since invading them in the 1240s. This got him his nickname.

"Terrible" is a translation of a Russian word that can also mean "awe-inspiring" or "great" – but Ivan certainly had a terrible temper. He apparently hit his eldest son so hard on the head in one of his rages that it killed him.

St Basil's Cathedral is one of the most famous symbols of Russia today. It was built by Ivan the Terrible.

Peter the Great

In 1613 Mikhail I became Russia's ruler. He was a member of the Romanov family, which ruled Russia for the next 300 years. One of the most famous Romanovs was Peter the Great who became tsar in 1682 when he was only ten. Peter grew to two metres tall, and was very energetic and determined to make Russia a modern country. He built a new capital city – St Petersburg – on Russia's northern coast. Having this port meant Russia was able to trade more with the West. Under the Romanovs Russia became a great power.

Peter the Great was a very energetic man and got involved with practical jobs like shipbuilding.

Why did the tsarist system last so long in Russia?

Just like European kings at the time, a tsar had absolute power over his people, most of whom were **serfs**. The tsarist system lasted much longer than similar systems in the West because Russia developed more slowly.

Revolution!

At the beginning of the 20th century Russia was still ruled by a tsar. The serfs had been freed in 1861 but the lives of most Russians were as harsh as ever. They wanted a say in how they were governed, but the tsar, Nicolas II, thought he knew what was best for them. Nicolas was a weak ruler, not up to governing the vast empire that Russia had become and made many mistakes. Protests, strikes, and an unsuccessful war against Japan finally forced Nicolas to grant his people a "duma", or parliament, but it had no real power.

Rasputin

Nicolas had advisers to help him govern. One of them was a Siberian monk, called Rasputin. Tsar Nicolas and Empress Alexandra came to rely on Rasputin, believing he could cure their son Alexei's haemophilia (a disease that makes it very hard to stop bleeding if you are cut). Rasputin became very powerful but was not trusted by the people, who blamed him for many of the bad decisions the tsar made.

This cartoon shows how people saw Rasputin, as a sinister figure dominating the weak tsar.

In 1914, Russia joined the First World War. It was a disaster. The soldiers were badly equipped and huge numbers of them died. At home there wasn't enough food for people to eat. More strikes and violent protests broke out and Nicolas was forced to **abdicate**. A temporary government took over the ruling of the country, but it was overthrown in 1917 by **revolutionaries** called Bolsheviks.

National tragedy

Millions of Russian soldiers were killed or wounded in the First World War.

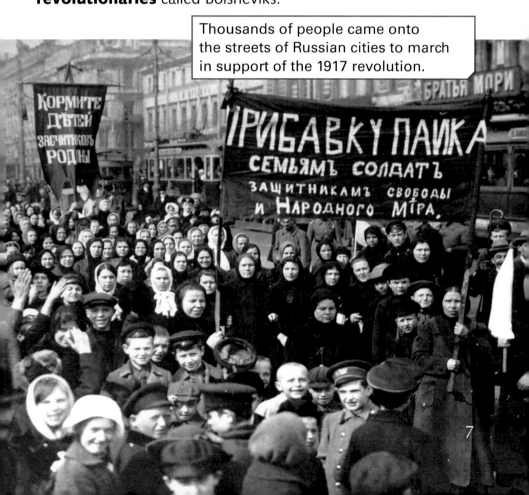

Thousands of people came onto the streets of Russian cities to march in support of the 1917 revolution.

Lenin and the Bolsheviks

"Peace, land and bread!" Vladimir Lenin, the Bolshevik Party leader, promised the Russian people. He took Russia out of the First World War, so it would no longer waste its strength on fighting.

Equal rights
The Bolsheviks worked to give women equal status with men, and celebrated their role in the revolution.

Lenin
Vladimir Lenin started as a violent revolutionary, but came to rule the newly formed Soviet Union. He wanted to help the poor, but he was ruthless towards anyone who opposed him.

Lenin giving a speech to workers in Red Square in 1917. The building behind him is the Kremlin, the home of the Russian government.

At the time there was a great division of wealth. Some Russians were enormously rich, but most were desperately poor. The Bolsheviks changed that, and declared that all property belonged to everyone equally. This idea is known as communism.

Lenin set up councils, known as soviets, to help the Bolsheviks stay in power. Not everyone wanted the Bolsheviks to rule Russia, however, and civil war broke out between the Bolsheviks (the "Reds") and their enemies (the "Whites"). Thousands of people were arrested and executed without trial. By 1922, the Bolsheviks had beaten their enemies, and Russia became the world's first communist country.

The tsar and his family were held captive by the Bolsheviks; then executed in July 1918.

Maria

Alexandra

Anastasia

Olga

Nicolas

Alexei

Tatiana

9

The Union of Soviet Socialist Republics (USSR)

Running the country

The Communists – as the Bolsheviks were known now – believed that people should be treated equally. Working conditions improved and everyone now had free education. However, for many people life was still very harsh. The long civil war caused food shortages and starvation in many parts of the country. You couldn't go to church because religion was banned, and if you spoke out against the government you were severely punished.

The Young Pioneers

The Young Pioneers Soviet youth movement was founded by Lenin and run like the Scouts. They even had a similar motto – "Always ready"!

Communal flats

The Bolsheviks seized the mansions that belonged to
the wealthy and divided them into apartments. This meant
that everyone now had somewhere to live, and encouraged
a communal lifestyle where everyone had to share.
People from different backgrounds lived side by side,
one family to a room, with everyone sharing the kitchen
and bathroom. Communal living lasted until the fall of
the USSR (also known as the Soviet Union) in 1991.

Being a Young Pioneer taught children to be adventurous and self-reliant.

Stalin's dictatorship

A ruthless dictator

When Lenin died in 1924, Joseph Stalin seized power. He was a dictator, a leader who had total control over the country and crushed all opposition, but he also transformed Russia.

Turning the country into an industrial superpower came at huge cost. Five-year plans were introduced to increase the output of factories. Individual farms were merged into giant **collective farms**. In Ukraine, which was part of the Soviet Union, around five million people starved to death as farmers' harvests were taken as punishment for refusing to join the collective farms.

Catching up with the neighbours

Huge projects like the building of the Dnieper dam helped modernise the Soviet Union.

Workers on collective farms were supposed to be strong, happy and eager to work.

Photographs and posters of Stalin showed him as a wise, fatherly man. In reality, he was cunning and ruthless.

The Great Terror

Stalin believed there were enemies everywhere. His secret police sent thousands of suspected enemies to a network of labour camps known as gulags, where they were forced to work building railways and canals, or in the mines. Many of the prisoners died or simply disappeared. This time was known as the Great Terror.

State first

13-year-old Pavlik Morozov reported his father to the authorities for betraying the state. He was used as an example to teach Soviet children that loyalty to the state was more important even than your family.

13

The Second World War

By 1938 many people thought there would be another war in Europe. Adolf Hitler (the leader of the Nazi party in Germany) wanted to take over lands he said belonged to Germany. Stalin did not want Russia to be drawn into another war, and made a secret agreement with Hitler that neither country would invade the other. This left Hitler free to invade Poland, which started the Second World War, while Stalin attacked Latvia, Estonia and Lithuania, making them part of the Soviet Union.

Lyudmila Pavlichenko

Lyudmila Pavlichenko was a sniper, famous for killing Nazis. In 1942, she toured the USA encouraging men to join the fight against **fascism.**

Lyudmila Pavlichenko killed over 300 enemies of Russia during the Second World War.

In 1941 Hitler broke his word and invaded Russia, quickly overrunning the west of the country. Now Russia joined the fight against Germany. It was a brutal war. The Russians were forbidden to surrender, which led to great suffering and the starvation of thousands in **besieged** cities like Leningrad (formerly St Petersburg). At the battle for Stalingrad – the bloodiest conflict of the war – the tide finally turned against Hitler, and in 1945 the Germans surrendered.

In Russia nine million soldiers and 18 million civilians had died.

What's in a name?

The city now called St Petersburg was called Leningrad from 1924 to 1991.

Every year on 9 May, Russians march to commemorate the Soviet Union's victory over Nazi Germany.

Cold War

A war without fighting

At the end of the Second World War, the Soviet Union controlled several Eastern European countries, and set up communist governments there. Western countries were worried. How many more countries would the Russians take over and turn into communist states? The Russians viewed the West with equal distrust. This began a long period called the Cold War, lasting from 1947 to 1985, in which East and West spied on each other, and the world's two "superpowers" – the USA and the USSR – competed to dominate the world. Both countries had **nuclear** weapons, and in 1962 they came close to launching them.

When Stalin died in 1953, millions of Russians were genuinely upset and filed past his body to pay their respects.

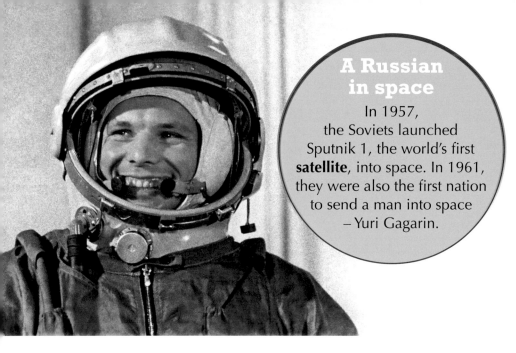

A Russian in space

In 1957, the Soviets launched Sputnik 1, the world's first **satellite**, into space. In 1961, they were also the first nation to send a man into space – Yuri Gagarin.

The KGB

The KGB was the Soviet Secret Service. It spied on the country's enemies and even on its own people.

The grim Lubyanka building was the headquarters of the KGB. Thousands of people were executed there.

The end of the USSR

Years of spending money on nuclear weapons, space technology and wars brought the Soviet **economy** to the brink of collapse. In 1985, the USSR's new leader, Mikhail Gorbachev, realised that something had to change. Two new **policies** called "glasnost" (openness) and "perestroika" (reconstruction) allowed people to talk openly about politics for the first time.

Chernobyl

In 1986, a nuclear power station at Chernobyl in Ukraine exploded, sending a poisonous cloud across the country and neighbouring states. The explosion was so terrible that the Soviet leadership began to question their policy of covering up problems.

The town of Pripyat was abandoned after the accident.

People had to queue for many hours just to buy basic things.

People began to question the system they'd lived under for so long, and there was much more cooperation between communist and Western countries. One by one, communist governments in Eastern Europe were overthrown, and finally Gorbachev allowed the republics that made up the USSR to hold free elections. In Russia, the biggest republic, the election was won by another **reformer** – Boris Yeltsin.

Boris Yeltsin addressed huge crowds of supporters during his 1989 election campaign.

Russia returns

Not everyone wanted the Soviet Union to break up. In August 1991, extreme communists attempted to push Gorbachev out of power and undo his reforms. Thousands of outraged people took to the streets and the extremists were forced to back down.

Many people in Russia were desperate for change.

Yeltsin the hero

Yeltsin famously climbed onto the top of a tank and urged the army not to attack the people.

The Soviet Union used a red flag with a hammer and sickle logo. In 1991, Russia went back to using its own flag.

On 25 December, Gorbachev **resigned**. The next day, the Soviet flag was taken down from the Kremlin for the last time. The Soviet Union no longer existed. Russia became a **democracy** for the first time in its history.

Yeltsin's reforms

Yeltsin was now president of Russia. He sold government-owned companies to businessmen, so the government would no longer have to be involved. Many people thought this change came too quickly and industries were sold too cheaply. As a result, a few people became hugely wealthy while life got harder for most others.

President Yeltsin visited many countries, including the USA. Here he is pictured with President George H. W. Bush and his wife at the White House in Washington D.C. in 1992.

21

Putin

Vladimir Putin became president of Russia in 1999. Although the government took back control of some industries during the 2000s, by the middle of the 2010s most large energy, farming and transport companies had been sold to businessmen.

Russian troops like these are still fighting wars on the country's borders.

Putin shows the Russian people that he's strong and physically fit – a tireless leader.

Wars

Not every republic wants to stay part of Russia. From 1994 to 2009, rebels fought a war to try to make Chechnya an independent country. In March 2014, Russia invaded the Crimea, a part of Ukraine, and declared that it was part of Russia.

Putin is very popular in Russia, especially in the countryside, and in 2012 he was elected president for the next six years. The tradition of strong leadership in Russia goes back to the time of the tsars, and people see Putin as strong and decisive.

How people live
Gas and oil

Russia has a lot of natural resources – useful materials that can be found underground, such as oil, copper and gas. Vast forests supply wood, and huge farms produce wheat and corn. Russia produces a lot of gas and oil and sells it to other countries.

In recent years, however, other countries have bought less of these things. This means Russia's economy has become weaker, and there's less money for important things like medical care, roads and pensions.

Diamonds

Russia is the world's biggest **exporter** of real and fake diamonds. Diamonds are not only beautiful, but very hard. They can even cut through rock and concrete.

There are over 600 billion trees in Russia, but they are being cut down at a very fast rate.

A huge tanker docking at one of the terminals run by a Russian oil company.

Russia still has a huge amount of oil and gas. However, it's mostly in remote regions like eastern Siberia, where the enormous distances and difficult conditions make drilling or digging to get them very costly. Russia can no longer sell these resources cheaply.

Russia produces huge amounts of wheat to export to other countries.

Tourism

A rich culture

Russia's wonderful history, culture and countryside make it popular with tourists. Major attractions include Red Square in Moscow, the Hermitage museum in St Petersburg and cross-country tours on the famous Trans-Siberian Express railway.

The Hermitage

The Hermitage is one of the world's great museums. It's housed in the 17th-century Winter Palace that was once the home of Russia's tsars. It contains almost three million works of art, ranging from Egyptian carvings to paintings by artists like Michelangelo and Matisse.

This amazing ceiling in the Hermitage is a copy of one painted by Italian artist Raphael in the early 1500s.

The Trans-Siberian Express goes past Lake Baikal.

The Trans-Siberian Express

The journey from Moscow to Vladivostok covers over 9,000 kilometres, takes seven days, and goes through both Europe and Asia. The construction of the line began in 1891, and several routes have been built. The full route from Moscow to Beijing in China opened in 1956. Passengers can travel on a standard train or take a luxury tour.

Red Square

Krasnaya Ploshchad, or Red Square, is the centre of Moscow, where parades, celebrations and official events take place. It's surrounded by famous landmarks like the 16th-century St Basil's Cathedral, and the Kremlin.

Rich and poor

In Russia, the gap between the very rich and the very poor is growing, like in tsarist times. Things have been made worse by problems like the big drop in the price of oil and Western governments' decision to trade less with Russia because they are worried the country may

Rich Russians enjoy luxurious lifestyles. Imagine eating your dinner here!

be unstable. There's less money to pay for public services, and wages and pensions are falling. Many jobs are part-time, meaning that life is uncertain for many people, especially the young.

Many Russian businessmen drive expensive foreign cars like this Porsche.

Not everyone is getting rich. There are many beggars in the streets of cities across Russia.

The oligarchs

The owners of the big companies that the government sold off in the 1990s are now very wealthy. They are known as "oligarchs" (very wealthy people). Although Putin has reduced the amount of political influence they have, oligarchs who are close to him still have enormous power.

City life

Before the Revolution, around 80% of Russians lived in the countryside. Stalin's programme of industrialisation drove people to the cities to work in the new factories. Apartment blocks in zones around the edges of cities were built to house them. By the end of the Soviet period, industrialised housing accounted for three-quarters of Russia's homes.

Well-off Russians often like to have richly decorated furniture in their homes.

apartment blocks for the rich in Russia

Poor urban Russians may live in run-down Soviet blocks like these.

Most city people still live in these blocks. Some are well-maintained and have good local shops, and nearby schools, parks and transport, but others urgently need repairs. Many blocks from the 1970s weren't built to last and are being demolished and new homes put up in their place.

Your own home

As rents are high, many Russians prefer to buy a home. Thousands of luxury flats are being built in big cities. But economic problems mean that only a few people can afford them.

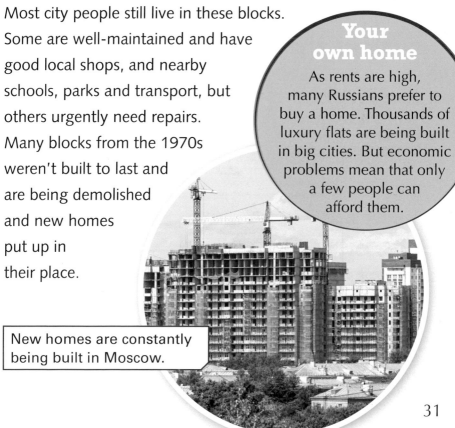

New homes are constantly being built in Moscow.

31

Country life

Left behind

Far fewer Russians live in the countryside nowadays compared to 100 years ago. Like in Soviet times, today's young Russians move to the cities where there are more jobs. The elderly people who remain may miss their neighbours and the old

Some villages still get their water from wells like this one.

communal way of life. Many countryside homes lack basic services like hot water and electricity. Few people have cars, and roads are seldom repaired. Local shops, schools and hospitals are often a long way away.

Traditional countryside houses are made of wood, like this one in the Novgorod area.

Dacha weekending

Many people enjoy visiting
the countryside, if not
living there. A lot of Russian
families spend summer
weekends and holidays in
a "dacha", a kind of cottage.
In Soviet times, most people's
dachas were simple log cabins
with a small garden where fruit and

Traditional
dachas are little
wooden buildings.

vegetables were grown. Nowadays, dachas can be big, with
more than one building and even a sauna! People staying in
dachas are welcomed in the countryside by villagers as they
have money to spend. Wealthy Russians might use their
dachas at weekends all year round.

Traditional Russian
saunas look
like this inside.
Note the huge stove
for making the room
toasty warm!

Russia's nomads

Only 10% of the tribes in Russia are still nomads, and move from place to place all their lives. Most are reindeer herders who live in the far north of the country, on frozen land known as tundra. There the land is grazed by the reindeer that supply people with food and hides they use for clothing, tents and other essential items.

Komi reindeer herders live in traditional tents that they carry around with them on dog sleds.

Reindeer hide coats keep the Nenets people warm all year round.

Until Soviet times, the nomads' way of life and traditions were respected. But under Stalin's policy of **collectivisation**, their land was taken away and the government tried to stop them speaking their own languages. They now face new threats from companies digging for oil and gas, tree-felling and global warming. There are also human threats. For example, in the Khanty-Mansiysk region of Siberia, the local parliament is removing the legal protection that prevents oil and gas companies from drilling without first asking the nomads' permission or respecting the environment.

Eating and drinking

Nowadays, Russians eat many of the same foods you'll find in any Western country, but there's still a place for traditional cooking. A family breakfast might include kasha (a kind of porridge) or kolbasa (sausage) and rye bread. Borscht (beetroup soup, served hot or cold) is a lunchtime favourite. Home-made pelmeni (a bit like Italian ravioli) are popular for lunch or dinner.

borscht
(beetroup soup)

Syrniki (cottage cheese pancakes) are a delicious breakfast treat!

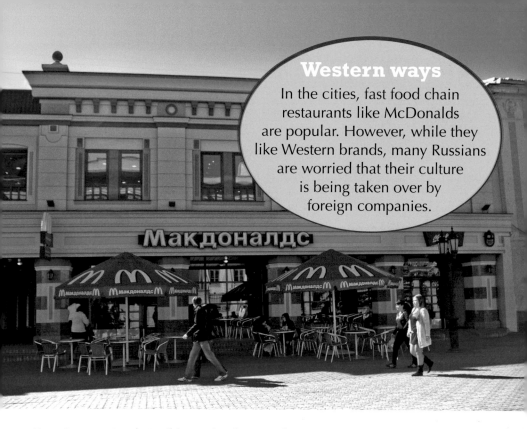

Western ways

In the cities, fast food chain restaurants like McDonalds are popular. However, while they like Western brands, many Russians are worried that their culture is being taken over by foreign companies.

Russians eat a lot of bread. This might be kalachi (buns) or little doughnuts called pyshki. Well-off Russians in the cities often eat out in restaurants, which wouldn't have been possible in Soviet times.

Tea is one of Russia's favourite drinks. It's traditionally made in a fancy pot called a samovar.

Schooldays

Education for all

Russians believe that education is very important, and all children aged six to 15 go to school. Many Russian schools have a school uniform. When they are 15, children take an exam, after which they either stay on at school for two more years and take more exams, or go to college for job training. To enter university, students must first pass the EGE (Unified State Exam).

Children usually attend a free local state school, though some parents who can afford it, send their children to boarding school abroad.

Learn your alphabet

The Russian alphabet has 33 letters and is called Cyrillic. Some of the letters are exactly the same as Roman (Western) ones, but others look the same and sound different!

Like Western children, Russians have to learn their ABC – except the first three letters in the Cyrillic alphabet are **АБВ** – which sounds like "ABV"!

38

Teenagers in the town of Ufa celebrate their graduation.

Knowledge Day

Returning to school on 1 September is an event to be celebrated in Russia. Children present flowers to their teachers, and teachers make speeches.

A Buryatian secondary schoolboy holds a younger student on his shoulders. The girl is ringing a hand bell, which is another tradition on Knowledge Day.

The school day

A Russian school day begins at around 8:30 a.m.
In Moscow, most children go to a local school, but some
go to schools further away. It can be a long journey on
the metro (the underground train) as there are large
distances between stops.

Children in a Russian village
wait with their teacher to
catch a bus to school.

A girl walks to school in the rural district of Tver.

The school day often begins with the head teacher giving a talk about the importance of good behaviour. The children are then taught most of the same subjects as children in Western countries. There are also specialist schools where they can study drama or music. The day ends in the early afternoon,

Kindergarten

Many Russian parents send their children to kindergarten to prepare them for primary school. Children take part in activities like music, art and sport, and perform plays for their parents.

although some children stay on for after-school activities.

Celebrations

Russians celebrate many special occasions. The most important is Novy God – New Year. Families spend the evening together and at midnight visit friends and neighbours. Special foods are eaten, like pierogi (stuffed dumplings), pickled mushrooms, and a special Russian salad. In the morning, children look under the New Year tree eager to see if Ded Moroz (Father Frost) and his granddaughter Snegurochka (Little Snow Girl) have been and brought them presents. The New Year tree is decorated with sweets and a star on top.

Russians celebrate New Year with firework displays, like this one in Moscow in 2012.

Ded Moroz and Snegurochka delivering presents to children

Christmas

Christmas was banned in Soviet times, but is now often celebrated as well as New Year. In Russia, Christmas Day falls on 7 January. Families go to church on Christmas Eve.

This big tree was put up in the centre of St Petersburg for New Year 2015.

Special days

Maslenitsa and Easter

Maslenitsa is probably the country's oldest festival, and is celebrated by Russians everywhere. In Russia, it lasts for the seven days before the Christian religious period of Lent begins. Pancakes called blinis are eaten – a last treat before Lent. At Easter, decorated eggs are popular. After going to church, families celebrate with a special Easter breakfast.

Maslenitsa involves eating pancakes, and also other foods such as sweet-tasting bread rings.

Burning a scarecrow is a traditional part of celebrating Maslenitsa.

44

These Russian Easter eggs are real eggs that have been carefully painted.

Happy birthday!

Russians think it's unlucky to celebrate a birthday before the day itself, so if a birthday happens in the week it's usually celebrated the following weekend. Children are given small gifts and have a party for their friends. A special sweet pie, stuffed with fruit, is often eaten instead of birthday cake. The child's name is carved on the pie crust. After eating, the children play games.

Name days

The Russian tradition of celebrating a saint's day for the person of that name was once as important as celebrating birthdays. The tradition ended after the 1917 revolution.

Sports and games
2018 World Cup

People are very excited about the 2018 World Cup, which will be held in Russia. Players from top Russian teams like Lokomotiv Moscow and Zenit St Petersburg are waiting to see who'll be selected to play.

Stadiums and training grounds are being built across the country, and young people are being helped to develop their football skills. Russians who've never been abroad are thrilled about getting the chance to see players from all around the world.

Zenit St Petersburg won the Russian Premier League in May 2015.

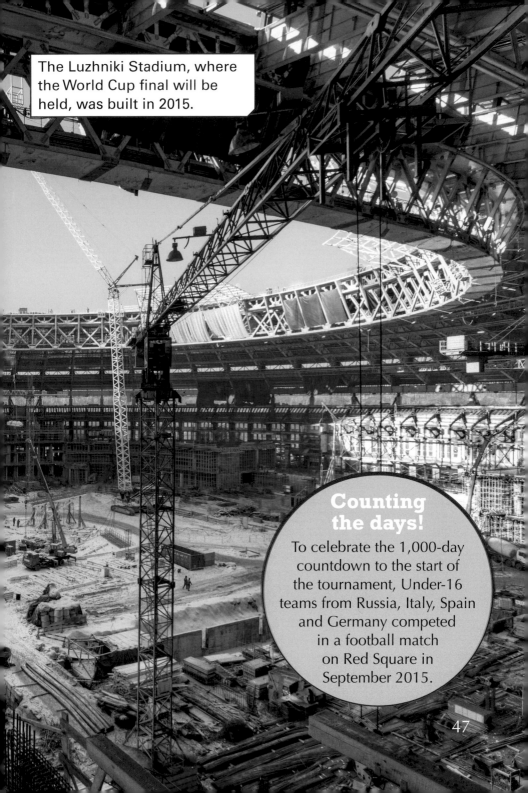

The Luzhniki Stadium, where the World Cup final will be held, was built in 2015.

Counting the days!

To celebrate the 1,000-day countdown to the start of the tournament, Under-16 teams from Russia, Italy, Spain and Germany competed in a football match on Red Square in September 2015.

Olympics and Paralympics

Land of achievers

Sport is important to Russians, and talented children often get the chance to become stars.

The Soviet Union first sent a team to compete in the Olympic Games in 1953. Since then, first the Soviet Union, and then Russia, have usually come top or near the top of the medal table. In the 2012 London Paralympic Games, the Russian team came second, and at the Winter Olympics in Sochi (a Russian town) in 2014, they came top. Sadly, it's since been found that some Russian athletes were taking drugs to improve their performance, but authorities are working to change the system so the country can compete fairly again.

a Russian skier in the jump event at the Sochi Winter Olympics in 2014

Olga Korbut

At the Olympic Games in Munich in 1972, a 17-year-old Soviet gymnast called Olga Korbut dazzled the audience with her performance. She won three gold medals and one silver, inspiring girls all around the world to take up the sport.

Olga Korbut's amazing performance at the 1973 European Gymnastic Championships

A sporting country

Tennis, chess, ice skating and ice hockey are some of Russia's favourite sports. Chess has been an important national game since tsarist times, but tennis has become popular in Russia only more recently. Stars like Maria Sharapova, Yevgeni Kafelnikov and Marat Safin have all been World Number One.

Russian Anna Kournikova and Swiss Martina Hingis winning the Australian Open Doubles in 2002

Russian ice hockey players are some of the best in the world.

In 2004, 17-year-old Maria Sharapova was the first Russian to win the Wimbledon Championships, by beating one of the greatest-ever female tennis players, Serena Williams. In 2008, the women's tennis team won gold, silver and bronze medals at the Olympics in Beijing.

Younger and younger

Russia has produced many talented figure skaters. Many start skating at the age of four. Some children as young as 12 have won major championships!

Chess Champions

Russia is famous for its chess geniuses. In 1983, Garry Kasparov became the youngest player ever to win the World Championship, at the age of 22.

Garry Kasparov defeating Viswanathan Anand in 1995.

Arts and entertainment

Russians love ballet. The country is home to many ballet companies, including two of the world's greatest – the Mariinsky in St Petersburg and the Bolshoi in Moscow. Both companies often take performances on tour around the world. Russia has also produced legendary dancers including Anna Pavlova, Vaslav Nijinsky and Rudolf Nureyev.

Famous Russian choreographer Sergei Diaghilev founded the Ballet Russes, which in spite of its name was based in Paris and never performed in Russia. The Ballet Russes is especially well-known for its production of Stravinsky's strange ballet *The Rite of Spring*, which was booed at its first performance in 1913.

Audiences in 1913 found *The Rite of Spring* strange and hard to understand.

Moscow State Circus

The world-famous Moscow State Circus was founded in the 18th century when an Englishman put on a show for Empress Catherine the Great. The empress was so impressed that she ordered two circus rings to be built. The circus's shows have themes inspired by Russian folk tales.

The Moscow State Circus performing on New Year's Day in Moscow 2012. The Circus is especially famous for its acrobatics.

Great writers and composers

Russia has a very rich culture.
Performances of classical music
written by Pyotr Tchaikovsky,
Sergei Rachmaninov and other
famous composers still attract big
audiences today.

the composer
Rachmaninov

Some of the world's most famous
plays, poems and novels were written
by Russian authors such as Leo Tolstoy,
Fyodor Dosloevsky, Alexander Pushkin and Anton Chekhov.
Author Alexander Solzhenitsyn bravely criticised communist
society at a time when it wasn't safe to do so. His book
The Gulag Archipelago describes what it was like to be
imprisoned in one of Stalin's labour camps.

Russia also has excellent authors
writing now, although, as few
of their works have been
translated, they aren't
well-known in the West.

a production of the opera
Boris Godunov by the
composer Mussorgsky

Pushkin – "Russia's Shakespeare"

Many people believe that Pushkin was Russia's greatest author. Pushkin was a poet, a novelist and a playwright. His most famous work is the poem *Eugene Onegin*. Tchaikovsky wrote an opera based on it.

Pushkin, who died in 1837, is the most respected writer in Russian history.

Plays and novels

The novels of Tolstoy and the plays of Chekhov are some of the most studied works of literature in the world.

a performance of *The Cherry Orchard*, a play by Chekhov

Folk arts and crafts

For centuries all over Russia, craftspeople have been carving wooden bears, weaving beautiful lace, and making blue and white pottery. But many traditional crafts are now disappearing. The work is badly paid, and many young people would rather find a better-paid job in the city or easier work in a shop.

a boy trying traditional Russian metalwork at a street festival in Vologda

Carpet-weaving is a traditional Russian craft.

Bogorodskoye carving

Wooden bears and other figures have been carved in the village of Bogorodskoye since at least the 17th century. They're often made from single pieces of wood.

It's increasingly difficult to sell traditional handmade products, as they're much more expensive than the mass-produced copies that are being made since the collapse of the Soviet Union. Shops sell the copies much more often than handmade originals.

Matryoshka

Perhaps the most well-known souvenir of trips to Russia is the matryoshka, a series of brightly painted dolls nesting one inside the other. People associate them with Russia, but they were actually first made in Japan!

57

Fabergé – jeweller to the tsars

In Russia, it's a tradition for families to give each other coloured eggs at Easter, but the eggs made by jeweller and goldsmith Peter Carl Fabergé for the royal family were made of gold and gems! He made the first one for Tsar Alexander III in 1885 to give to his wife, and it was so successful that each Easter until the Revolution, Fabergé made special eggs for the royal family.

The first egg made by Fabergé for Tsar Alexander III was called the Hen Egg. Inside is a golden hen hiding a tiny crown made of rubies and diamonds. All Fabergé eggs hid a tiny surprise like this!

Anniversary egg

In 1913, Tsar Nicolas II gave his wife Alexandra a special Fabergé egg, celebrating the 300 years that his family had ruled Russia.

Carl Fabergé at the Hermitage Museum

Fabergé was able to study the Hermitage's works of art, which helped inspire his own creations. Now many of the objects he made are exhibited at the Hermitage, but the famous eggs are housed in another museum in St Petersburg, the Shuvalov Palace.

In 1918, the Bolsheviks seized Fabergé's eggs and stored them in the Kremlin. Later, Stalin sold them abroad to raise money. Most of the eggs are now in private collections and museums around the world, but some are back in Russia. Of the 50 eggs made for the tsars, seven are still missing.

21st-century egg

In 2014, President Putin presented the Hermitage with a Fabergé egg, to celebrate the museum's 250th anniversary.

Everyday life

Transport

Owning a car is a sign of social status in Russia and many city-dwellers drive rather than take public transport. However, increasing car use in cities has led to traffic jams, and plans to deal with the problem – such as bike and bus lanes – get little funding compared to big projects like ring roads and railways.

Outside the cities, people prefer trains, because roads are poor and car accidents are common. People sometimes have to fly to reach remote regions. However, many airports have closed, making transport to some areas very difficult.

High-speed commuter trains run between Moscow and St Petersburg.

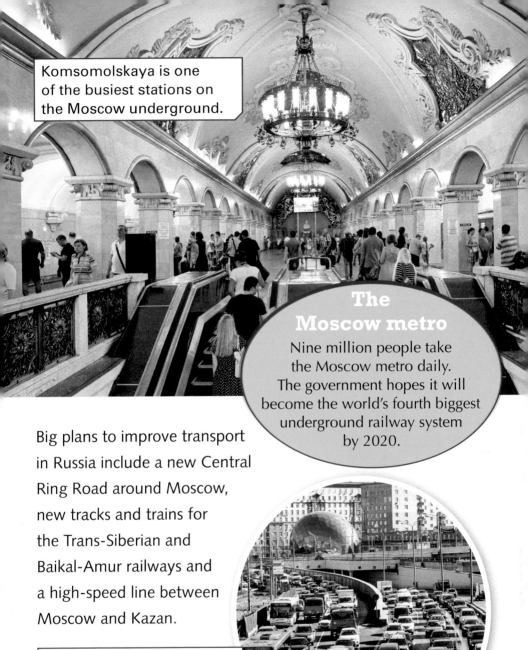

Komsomolskaya is one of the busiest stations on the Moscow underground.

The Moscow metro

Nine million people take the Moscow metro daily. The government hopes it will become the world's fourth biggest underground railway system by 2020.

Big plans to improve transport in Russia include a new Central Ring Road around Moscow, new tracks and trains for the Trans-Siberian and Baikal-Amur railways and a high-speed line between Moscow and Kazan.

Traffic jams are a major problem in Russian cities.

Communications

In Soviet times, radio, television, telephones and newspapers were all controlled by the government. Now most Russians in cities are able to communicate with each other by mobile phone and email. Communication is less easy in the countryside, but improvements are planned so that everyone will have better connections. Use of mobile phones is expected to grow hugely. By 2017, around 122 million Russians are expected to have their own mobile.

City-living Russians are now as plugged into their mobile phones and tablets as people in the West.

Popov and the radio

Russians are particularly proud of Alexander Popov, an important inventor of radio, so they celebrate Radio Day each year.

an early Popov radio

Russians watch a lot of TV. They can choose programmes from a wide variety of channels, including ones especially for children. Foreign TV and films are also popular, and they can be watched on the internet.

Healthcare

The government is supposed to supply free healthcare to all Russians, but resources are tight. In the first years after the fall of the USSR, a lot of money was put into the public healthcare system. However, because of economic problems there's now less money available, so the government is trying to make the system more efficient by closing small clinics and spending its money on big hospitals instead.

elderly patients being treated in a village clinic

Many Russians oppose the changes to healthcare. The people here are campaigning for better treatment.

Many health professionals have lost their jobs and others are working longer hours. Patients often have to pay for their medicines, and even treatments for serious conditions like cancer. Russians who can afford it are choosing to pay for their care with expensive private health insurance. When you have insurance, you pay a certain amount of money to an insurance company every year, and in return they pay for any medical treatment you need.

65

The environment

Russia – a land of contrast

Russia has many different kinds of land and climates – vast icy wastes in the far north, the largest forests in the world, huge plains, deserts, marshes, mountains, seas, rivers, lakes and volcanoes. The treeless steppe – a kind of plain – stretch for thousands of kilometres, while in other regions sandy deserts, icy mountains and forests meet.

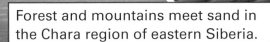

Forest and mountains meet sand in the Chara region of eastern Siberia.

In Russia, the summers are usually short and the winters long. In different parts of the country, temperatures can reach a scorching 40 degrees centigrade in summer and dip as low as −60 degrees centigrade in winter! This means there are many different environments, where different animals live. Unfortunately, many of them are endangered because of human activity.

Rare species like the Arctic fox live in the far north of Russia.

a smoking volcano in Kamchatka, the country's most volcanic region

Tundra, taiga and steppe

The tundra of the north

The far north of Russia extends into the Arctic Circle.
For much of the year, the ground there is frozen hard.
This frozen land is known as "tundra". In summer,
the ground becomes boggy, and plants like moss provide

food for reindeer, which
are the largest animals that
can survive there. Even in
summer, the temperature
is often around freezing,
and it seldom gets above
12 degrees centigrade.

A lot of familiar Arctic animals
live in the far north of Russia.

Taiga forest

Russia's great taiga forests
are found in lowlands and
on mountainsides south
of the treeless tundra.
The trees are mostly conifers
– pine, spruce and fir – which
means their needles contain
little sap and don't freeze in
icy temperatures. The larch is
the one other tree that can survive the harsh climate. The taiga
is home to creatures like foxes, bears and deer.

Majestic brown bears
live in the taiga.

Steppe

The steppe is a vast plain that stretches across much of
southern Russia. Not much rain falls here, which means that
only grasses can grow.

white feather grass
growing on the steppe

69

Threats to the environment

Russia has a lot of natural resources such as oil, gas, copper and lead. These are very important for Russia's economy, but the process of getting them out of the earth damages the environment and the wildlife.

Pollution is a major problem. There are now so many cars in the country that vehicles cause even more pollution than industry does. Many people have no safe drinking water.

Lake Baikal

Russia's Lake Baikal is the world's deepest lake. It contains one-fifth of the world's fresh water, but some experts say it's in danger of becoming a swamp.

Lake Baikal is becoming increasingly polluted.

As the ice in the north melts, polar bears find it hard to hunt.

Urengoy

Russia is home to some of the world's largest natural gas fields, such as Urengoy in Siberia.

Building, logging and poaching are other major threats to the environment. So is global warming. Human activities, like burning oil, release a gas called carbon dioxide into the air, and this gas traps heat near the surface of the planet. In cold countries like Russia, this means that the sea ice and **permafrost** are melting.

As the climate warms up, red foxes are taking over the Arctic foxes' territory.

Protecting wildlife

Russia has the biggest system of protected areas in the world, although they cover only a small part of the country. There are 105 of them, and they protect different types of habitats and the creatures that live in them.

The first one was set up near Lake Baikal in 1916 and covers part of the lake, plus the nearby mountains and forest.

Some protected areas are only the size of a few football pitches, but others are vast. Many are wild and beautiful. Some of them are now under threat, as central government has reduced the level of protection they get. More and more tourists visit these remote spots, which could damage or destroy important habitats.

Russia has 44 national parks.
This is the Yugyd-Va National Park
in the Ural mountains.

The Siberian tiger

Siberian tigers have almost died out because of poaching, logging, and building on their habitat. The World Wildlife Fund and the Russian government have been trying to save them, and in 2015 there were about 500 tigers, an increase of 50 since 2005.

Siberian tigers are an endangered species.

bison grazing in a nature reserve

Forwards to the future

Russia today

Russia today faces many challenges and economic difficulties, but it remains rich in natural resources, culture and history. It has a lot of influence in the world, and is a prominent member of important international organisations like the United Nations.

In 2018, Russia will host the World Cup, which will bring lots of visitors to the country as well as jobs. Transport, hotels, roads, sports grounds and airports will all be improved.

It's a chance for Russia to show the world all it has to offer, and to bring its people together to create a better future for everyone.

Putin with German leader Angela Merkel at a recent meeting of world leaders

Russia 20 years on

Try to imagine that you're living in Russia 20 years from now. What sort of country do you think it might be? Will Russia continue to have a big influence on the world?

people protesting against election results in December 2011

Glossary

abdicate　to give up ruling a country

besieged　trapped by an invading army

collective farms　individual farms merged into one large one that is owned by the state

collectivisation　taking people's goods and property to make a single large operation run by the state for the people

democracy　a country that is ruled by a government voted for by the country's people in free elections

economy　a country's wealth and resources that are managed by its government

exporter　a country that makes goods to sell in another country

federation　a united group of countries

nuclear　power that comes from smashing atoms, and which can be used to power countries' electricity supply or make destructive bombs or missiles.

permafrost　a layer of soil under the surface that remains frozen all year round in some parts of the world

policies　programmes of action

pollution　harmful substances in the atmosphere

reformer　someone who wants to improve a system

republics　countries that are ruled by governments voted for by the country's people, within the limits of certain laws, and have an elected president

resigned　gave up a job

revolutionaries　people who want to overthrow a government by violent means

satellite　a man-made object orbiting (circling) around the Earth in space

serfs　people forced to work their masters' land for no pay, rather like slaves

tsar　a Russian ruler with absolute power over his people

Index

Russian history timeline

1240s
Mongol invaders conquer southern Russia.

1550s
Ivan the Terrible defeats the Mongols and unites Russia.

1500   1600   1700   1800

around 500 CE
Slavic and Rus peoples settle in the country we now call Russia.

1682
Peter the Great becomes tsar – he modernises Russia and makes it a great empire.

1917
The Russian
Revolution ends
tsarist rule.
The Bolsheviks take
power and
Russia becomes
a communist country.

1947–1985
the Cold War –
a period when
the USSR and
the USA compete
to dominate
the world

1991
the fall of
the USSR

1900

2000

1924–1953
Joseph Stalin
industrialises Russia,
and rules by terror.

1985
Mikhail Gorbachev
becomes Soviet leader and
gives people more freedom.

1999
Vladimir Putin becomes
president of Russia.

Ideas for reading

Written by Clare Dowdall, PhD
Lecturer and Primary Literacy Consultant

Reading objectives:
- explore the meaning of words in context
- ask questions to improve their understanding
- summarise the main ideas drawn from more than one paragraph, identifying key details that support the main ideas

Spoken language objectives:
- articulate and justify answers, arguments and opinions
- give well-structured descriptions, explanations and narratives for different purposes

Curriculum links: History – place knowledge

Resources: atlas, ICT for research, pencil and paper, materials for making model Fabergé eggs

Build a context for reading
- Look at the front cover and ask children to share what they know about Russia. Collect the information in a spidergram.
- Read the blurb together. Add more information to the spidergram, supporting children to make inferences and deductions from the information provided, e.g. beautiful architecture, tea drinking.
- Locate Russia in an atlas. Note its location in relation to Europe and Asia.
- Turn to the contents. Ask children to choose a chapter that interests them and predict what sorts of information might be featured in it.

Understand and apply reading strategies
- Read pp2–3 together. Discuss how Russia is organised and model how to check the meaning of *federation* and *republics* using the glossary.